Even·
of 19⌣⌣

News for every day of the year

**US President Franklin Delano Roosevelt
arrives at his inauguration ceremony,
4 March 1933.**

By Hugh Morrison

MONTPELIER PUBLISHING

Front cover (clockwise from left): The airship USS *Macon* crosses the USA on 16 October. The film *King Kong* is released on 2 March. The Chicago World's Fair opens on 27 May. Mahatma Gandhi begins a fast in support of Untouchables on 8 May. Film star Jean Harlow marries for the third time on 18 September.The first issue of *Newsweek* magazine is published on 17 February.

Back cover (clockwise from top): The Anglo-Japanese Alliance is renewed on 27 October. George Orwell's seminal book *Down and Out in Paris and London* is published on 9 January. The Marx Brothers' comedy *Duck Soup* is released on 17 November. Adolf Hitler becomes Chancellor of Germany on 30 January. The Loch Ness Monster is purportedly photographed for the first time on 12 November. Popeye the Sailor Man makes his first screen appearance on 14 July. The *Hotspur* comic is first published on 2 September.

Image credits: US Navy, Mikroscops, Ron Kroon, NASA, Larry Philpot.

Published in Great Britain by Montpelier Publishing.
Printed and distributed by Amazon KDP.
This edition © 2022. All rights reserved.

ISBN: 9798841848509

January
1933

Sunday 1: The Soviet Union begins its second Five Year Plan, aiming to double its gross domestic product by 1937.

The seven-year-long American occupation of Nicaragua ends.

Capital punishment is abolished in Denmark.

Monday 2: Franklin D. Roosevelt ends his term as Governor of New York.

Tuesday 3: Japanese troops attack Jehol Province in China.

The Bitter Tea of General Yen starring Barbara Stanwyck becomes the first film to be shown at New York's Radio City Music Hall.

Nils Asther and Barbara Stanwyck star in the first film shown at the Radio City Music Hall on 3 January.

Wednesday 4: 19 people die when the French liner *L'Atlantique* catches fire in the English Channel.

A counterfeit plot by communists in the USA is uncovered, led by a respected New York physician Dr Gregory Burtan, who is

January 1933

sentenced to 15 years' imprisonment.

Thursday 5: All citizens of the USSR aged over 16 are required to carry an internal passport, controlling their movements within the country.

Construction of San Francisco's Golden Gate Bridge begins.

Calvin Coolidge, the only living US ex-President at this date, dies aged 60.

Friday 6: The gangster Clyde Barrow first achieves notoriety when he kills a police officer in Dallas, Texas.

Former US President Calvin Coolidge dies on 5 January.

Saturday 7: The Australian aviator Bert Hinkler dies aged 40 when his plane crashes in Italy during a round-the-world flying attempt.

Sunday 8: 21 people are killed during an anarchist uprising in Catalonia, Spain.

Monday 9: The author Eric Arthur Blair publishes his book *Down and Out in Paris and London*, his first work using the pen name George Orwell.

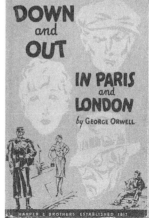

Left: the influential social critique, *Down and Out in Paris and London* by Eric Blair (George Orwell) is published on 9 January.

The novelist Wilbur Smith is born in Broken Hill, Rhodesia (died 2021).

Tuesday 10: Street fighting breaks out in Berlin, Germany, between Nazis and communists.

The actor Anton Rodgers (*Fresh Fields*) is born in Wisbech, Cambridgeshire (died 2007).

Wednesday 11: The first commercial flight takes place between Australia and New Zealand.

Thursday 12: 22 people are killed during fighting between anarchists and government troops in Casas Viejas, Spain.

Friday 13: The Russian aircraft manufacturing company Ilyushin is founded.

Above: Australian cricketer Bill Woodfull is injured by the new 'bodyline' bowling technique on 14 January.

Saturday 14: England defeats Australia 341-109 in cricket's Third Test at the Adelaide Oval; Australia's Bill Woodfull is injured by England's controversial 'bodyline' bowling technique.

Sunday 15: An apparition of the Virgin Mary is said to have appeared in the village of Banneux, Belgium.

Monday 16: Soviet leader Joseph Stalin orders the eviction of thousands of independent farmers (known as Kulaks) in order to seize their farms.

Miriam Ferguson becomes the first female governor of Texas on 17 January.

Tuesday 17: The US senate votes to grant independence to the Philippines within ten years.

January 1933

'Old Ironsides', shown here passing through the Panama Canal, begins a US coastal tour on 21 January.

Miriam 'Ma' Ferguson becomes the first woman governor of the state of Texas, and the second to serve as a US governor.

Wednesday 18: The US Department of Labor begins a campaign to deport film actors working illegally in the USA.

Thursday 19: The Irish aviatrix Lady Mary Bailey is found four days after crash landing in the deserts of Niger while flying from England to South Africa.

Friday 20: Paraguayan and Bolivian troops clash in the Battle of Nanawa.

Saturday 21: The USS *Constitution* ('Old Ironsides'), the first American battleship dating from 1797, begins a coastal tour of the USA.

Sunday 22: As the Ukranian famine worsens, Soviet authorities prevent all peasants from leaving the Ukraine; the sale of railway tickets is banned and barricades are erected around villages.

Monday 23: The Twentieth Amendment to the US Constitution changes the inauguration of the President from 4 March to 20 January.

Tuesday 24: Eamon de Valera's *Fianna Fail* party wins the general election in the Irish Free State.

Right: Marlene Dietrich causes a stir on 27 January when she appears in male attire.

January 1933

Far left: Adolf Hitler becomes Chancellor of Germany on 30 January.

Left: Édouard Deladier becomes Prime Minister of France on 29 January.

Wednesday 25: Corrie Aquino, 11th President of the Philippines, is born in Paniqui, Philippines. (died 2009).

Thursday 26: The League of Nations intervenes to prevent Peru from invading Colombia.

Friday 27: Film star Marlene Dietrich causes a sensation when she attends a Los Angeles film premiere dressed in a man's evening suit.

Saturday 28: Kurt von Schleicher resigns as Chancellor of Germany.

Joseph Paul Boncour resigns as Prime Minister of France.

The writer Choudhary Rahmat Ali coins the name 'Pakistan' for a separatist Muslim state in India. The name is taken from the initials of Punjab, Afghanistan, Kashmir and Sind.

Sunday 29: Édouard Deladier becomes Prime Minister of France.

Monday 30: Adolf Hitler becomes Chancellor of Germany.

The Lone Ranger makes his first appearance, in a radio programme broadcast by station WXYZ in Detroit.

Tuesday 31: The novelist John Galsworthy (*The Forsyte Saga*) dies aged 65.

February
1933

Wednesday 1: Adolf Hitler makes his first speech as Chancellor of Germany, pledging to end unemployment by 1937; the goal is achieved by 1936.

Thursday 2: *The Lone Ranger* becomes a regular series on syndicated US radio; it runs until 1954.

Friday 3: The musical comedy film *Hallelujah I'm a Bum* starring Al Jolson is released.

Saturday 4: Adolf Hitler bans any publications which are a 'threat to public order.'

Sunday 5: The Dutch navy mutinies at Sumatra.

Monday 6: The lowest recorded temperature in a town to this date is recorded at Oymyakon, Siberia. (-90.4F/-68C).

The TV personality Leslie Crowther (*The Price is Right*) is born

Above: The Boeing 247 first flies on 8 February.

in West Bridgeford, Nottinghamshire (died 1996).

Tuesday 7: A record-breaking wave of 112ft (34m) is recorded by the crew of the USS *Ramapo* in the Pacific Ocean.

Wednesday 8: The prototype of the Boeing 247, the first modern airliner, makes its maiden flight.

Adolf Hitler announces his goal of the complete rearmament of Germany within five years.

Above: Brace Beemer plays the Lone Ranger, who makes his first radio appearance on 2 February.

Thursday 9: The Oxford Union carries the controversial motion 'this house will in no circumstances fight for its King and Country' by 275-153 votes. A later historian records that most of those present go on to fight in the Second World War.

Friday 10: The first 'singing telegrams' are launched in the USA.

The heavyweight boxer Ernie Schaff is knocked out by Primo Carnera in a bout at New York's Madison Square Garden; he dies four days later aged 24.

Left to right: Frank Morgan, Edgar Conner and Al Jolson in a scene from the film *Halleluljah I'm a Bum*, released on 3 February.

February 1933

Far left: Kim Novak is born on 13 February.

Left: Yoko Ono is born on 18 February.

Saturday 11: The USA's Death Valley National Park is created.

Sunday 12: Sir William Robertson, Chief of Britain's Imperial General Staff in the First World War, dies aged 73. He is the only soldier in the British Army to have risen from the rank of private to Field Marshal.

Monday 13: The Warsaw Convention governing international air travel goes into effect.

The actress Kim Novak (*Vertigo*) is born in Eagle Point, Oregon.

Tuesday 14: All banks in Michigan are closed to prevent an impending run; the closures spread to many other banks across the USA.

Wednesday 15: Guiseppe Sangara attempts to assassinate US President Elect Franklin D Roosevelt; he is unhurt but Anton Cermak, Mayor of Chicago, is fatally wounded in the attack.

Left: Sir William Robertson, the only soldier in the history of the British Army to rise from the lowest rank of private to the highest of Field Marshal, dies on 12 February.

Thursday 16: Czechoslovakia, Romania and Yugoslavia sign a military pact to enforce the Little Detente, an alliance against a possible resurgence of the Austro-Hungarian Empire.

Friday 17: The first issue of *Newsweek* magazine is published.

Saturday 18: Yoko Ono, wife of John Lennon, is born in Tokyo, Japan.

Sir Bobby Robson, footballer and manager of the English national side, is born in Sacriston, County Durham (died 2009)

Sunday 19: The Vultee V1 single engined airliner makes its maiden flight.

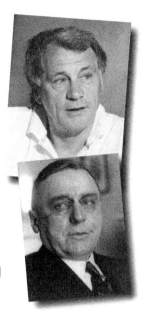

Top: Bobby Robson is born on 18 February. Above: Chicago mayor Anton Cermak is fatally wounded on 15 February.

Above: *Newsweek* magazine is first published on 17 February. Right: Nina Simone is born on 21 February.

Monday 20: Adolf Hitler holds a secret meeting with 25 leading German industrialists to raise funds for a Nazi election campaign.

Tuesday 21: The jazz singer Nina Simone is born in Tryon, North Carolina (died 2003).

February 1933

Above: The Reichstag on fire, 27 February.

Wednesday 22: Adolf Hitler authorises the construction of the first concentration camps for political prisoners.

Katharine, Duchess of Kent, the first member of the British Royal Family to convert to Roman Catholicism since 1701, is born in Hovingham Hall, Yorkshire.

Frances Perkins becomes the first woman to serve in the United States Cabinet.

Thursday 23: The Soviet Union bans foreign journalists from travelling anywhere outside Moscow.

Friday 24: Japan leaves the League of Nations after it is condemned for its occupation of Manchuria.

Saturday 25: The USS *Ranger,* the first purpose built aircraft carrier in the US Navy, is launched.

Sunday 26: Work begins on the foundations of the Golden Gate Bridge in San Francisco.

Monday 27: The German Reichstag (Parliament building) is destroyed in an arson attack. Blamed on communist subversives, the fire is thought to have been started by Nazi Party members as a pretext to increase Hitler's powers.

Tuesday 28: Following the Reichstag fire, Germany's President, Paul von Hindenburg, signs a decree suspending freedom of the press and rights of assembly and association. Nazi stormtroopers carry out mass arrests of suspected subversives across the country.

England's cricket team wins the Ashes against Australia.

March 1933

Wednesday 1: The fictional attorney-detective, Perry Mason, makes his first appearance in print, in the Earle Stanley Gardner novel *The Case of the Velvet Claws.*

Thursday 2: The action film *King Kong*, starring Fay Wray, is released. Famous for its stop-motion special effects, the film grosses $100,000 in its first week, saving RKO Pictures from bankruptcy.

Friday 3: 3000 people are killed when an earthquake and tsunami hit the Japanese island of Honshu.

Above, right: the action film *King Kong* is released on 2 March.

Right: Perry Mason makes his first appearance in *The Case of the Velvet Claws* on 1 March.

March 1933

Fascism on the rise: far left: Englebert Dollfuss suspends Austria's Parliament on 7 March.

Left: Joseph Goebbels sets up Germany's Propaganda Ministry on 11 March.

Saturday 4: Franklin Delano Roosevelt is sworn in as the 32nd President of the USA.

Sunday 5: In the last multi-party election in German until after the Second World War, Adolf Hitler's Nazi Party is victorious.

Monday 6: As the US financial crisis worsens, President Roosevelt declares a state of emergency and a compulsory bank holiday; gold exports and payments are banned.

General Nikolaos Plastiris seizes control of Greece in a military coup. He is deposed the following day by General Alexandros Othonaios.

Above: actor Michael Caine, shown here in 1967, is born on 13 March.

Tuesday 7: The Manchester United footballer Jackie Blanchflower, one of the survivors of 1958 Munich air disaster, is born in Belfast (died 1998).

The Austrian Chancellor, Englebert Dollfuss, suspends Parliament and begins to rule dictatorially.

Wednesday 8: As Prohibition draws to a close in the USA, the FBI announces it will no longer raid illegal drinking clubs (speakeasies).

Thursday 9: Nazi paramilitaries seize control of the German state of Bavaria.

Friday 10: 117 die when a 6.4 magnitude earthquake hits Long Beach, California.

Saturday 11: Germany's ministry of Nazi propaganda is set up under Joseph Goebbels.

Sunday 12: Six British aeronautical engineers are arrested in Moscow on espionage charges.

US President Roosevelt gives the first of his series of 28 'fireside chats' on the radio, explaining his reasons for imposing a state of emergency on 6 March.

Monday 13: 41 die in a fire in a theatre in Ahualulco de Mercado, Mexico.

The musician Mike Stoller, composer of hits including *Hound Dog* and *Jailhouse Rock*, is born in New York City (died 2011).

Tuesday 14: The American compulsory bank holiday ends, following the failure of 447 banks.

The actor Sir Michael Caine (Maurice Micklewhite) is born in London.

Left: US President Franklin D Roosevelt gives the first of his 'fireside chats' on the radio, 12 March.

March 1933

КРАСНЫЙ ПАХАРЬ

Left: a Soviet recruitment poster for collective farms. Despite the romantic propaganda, peasants are banned from leaving the farms on 18 March.

Wednesday 15: The seizure of grain for export from Ukrainian farmers is halted in the USSR, after the region experienced the crippling famine known as the Holodomor.

The actor Cary Grant is injured when a pyrotechnic device explodes on the set of the film *The Eagle and the Hawk.*

Thursday 16: Theodore Roosevelt Jr, cousin of US President FD Roosevelt, steps down as Governor of the Philippines.

Friday 17: Hjalmar Schact becomes Adolf Hitler's chief economic advisor.

The children's author Penelope Lively (*A Stitch in Time*) is born in Cairo, Egypt.

Saturday 18: The USSR bans peasants from leaving collective farms.

Sunday 19: In a constitutional referendum, the Prime Minister of Portugal, Antonio Salazar, is granted wide-ranging dictatorial powers. He rules the country until 1968.

Right: Antonio Salazar.

Above: the first political prisoners arrive in Germany's newly opened Dachau concentration camp, 22 March.

The Pulitzer Prize winning author Philip Roth is born in Newark, New Jersey (died 2018).

Monday 20: Guiseppe Zangara, who killed Chicago mayor Anton Cernak while attempting to assassinate President Franklin Roosevelt, is executed in Florida state prison.

Tuesday 21: Germany's Reichstag is formally reopened on Potsdam Day in a ceremony attended by Adolf Hitler, President Hindenburg and former Crown Prince Wilhelm.

Wednesday 22: The first German concentration camp, at Dachau, receives its first prisoners.

As Prohibition winds down, the US government approves the sale of beer of up to 3.2% alcohol.

Thursday 23: The German parliament passes the Enabling Act, allowing Adolf Hitler to assume dictatorial powers.

Friday 24: The first high strength industrial plastic, Low Density Polyethylene is created by British chemists Reginald Gibson and Eric Fawcett.

March 1933

Above: The USS *Sequoia*.

Saturday 25: The USS *Sequoia* becomes the official US Presidential yacht, with special adaptations for the wheelchair-bound President Roosevelt.

Sunday 26: The US State Department announces its findings in an enquiry into the maltreatment of Jews in Germany. It concludes the practice has 'virtually terminated.'

Monday 27: A one-day boycott of Jewish businesses is announced by the Nazi party in Germany.

Japan announces it will leave the League of Nations.

Tuesday 28: 15 people are killed when an Armstrong Whitworth Argosy airliner crashes near Brussels, Belgium.

Wednesday 29: Germany reinstates the death penalty.

The Welsh journalist Gareth Jones makes the first report to the world of the famine in the Ukraine.

Thursday 30: 68 die when tornadoes hit the southeastern USA.

Friday 31: All Jewish judges and lawyers in the German states of Prussia and Bavaria are ordered to resign.

The Civilian Conservation Corps is established in the USA to provide work for the unemployed.

Reporter Gareth Jones breaks the news of the Soviet famine cover-up on 29 March.

April
1933

Saturday 1: The first squadron of the newly formed Royal Indian Air Force is commissioned.

England cricketer Wally Hammond sets a record of 336 not out during a Test Match against New Zealand at Eden Park, Auckland.

Sunday 2: Siam (Thailand) passes legislation to control the spread of communism.

Monday 3: Dr Yuri Voronoy of the USSR performs the first kidney transplant; the recipient dies two days later due to incompatible blood groups.

The badge of the Royal Indian Air Force, which goes into use on 1 April.

Lord Clydesdale and Flight Lieutenant DF MacIntyre make the first flight over Mount Everest.

Michigan becomes the first US state to repeal Prohibition.

Tuesday 4: 73 die when the airship USS *Akron* crashes during storms 20 miles off the coast of New Jersey.

The German government orders the expulsion of Jews from most government jobs.

April 1933

Wally Hammond scores a record 336 not out on 1 April.

Wednesday 5: US President Roosevelt declares it illegal for Americans to own gold. All citizens are ordered to redeem gold at the set price of $20.67 per ounce.

Dr Evarts Graham of Washington University, St Louis, Missouri, performs the first pneumonectomy (removal of part of the lung).

Thursday 6: The Screen Writers' Guild is formed in the USA.

Friday 7: Beer goes on sale legally in 19 of 48 US states as Prohibition draws to a close.

Saturday 8: Western Australia votes in a referendum for independence; the British government concludes the referendum cannot be honoured without the approval of the Australian federal government, which is not forthcoming.

Sunday 9: The French film actor Jean-Paul Belmondo is born in Neuilly-sur-Seine (died 2021).

Monday 10: Pope Pius XI meets with senior Nazis Herman Goering and Fritz von Papen in Rome.

Tuesday 11: The British aviator William Lancaster goes missing while attempting to break the air speed record from London to Cape Town. His body is eventually found in the Sahara Desert in 1962.

Jean-Paul Belmondo is born on 9 April.

Wednesday 12: Sound engineer Harvey Fletcher demonstrates stereophonic sound for the first time, in Philadelphia, PA.

Adelbert Ames, the last surviving general to have served in the American Civil War, dies aged 97.

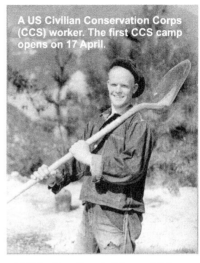

A US Civilian Conservation Corps (CCS) worker. The first CCS camp opens on 17 April.

Thursday 13: The first confirmed flight of a steam-powered aircraft takes place in Oakland, California. Many steam-powered planes were built in the nineteenth century but none successfully flew. Due to advances in petrol engine technology, by 1933 the idea of steam-powered flight is redundant.

Friday 14: After driving along the A82 in Scotland, Mr and Mrs John Mackay of Drumndrochit report the sighting of a strange aquatic creature in Loch Ness. The press takes an interest, and the world is introduced to the Loch Ness Monster.

Saturday 15: The actress Elizabeth Montgomery (*Bewitched*) is born in Los Angeles (died 1995).

Sunday 16: US racing driver Bob Carey is killed aged 28 at Legion Ascot Speedway, California.

The broadcaster Joan Bakewell is born in Stockport, Lancashire.

Monday 17: The first Civilian Conservation Corps camp is opened in the USA at Luray, Virginia, offering forestry work to the unemployed.

Tuesday 18: Romanian fascists injure 100 in attacks on Jewish businesses.

Pilot William Lancaster goes missing on 11 April during a speed record attempt.

April 1933

Above: Jayne Mansfield (shown here in 1957) is born on 19 April.

Wednesday 19: The US dollar is taken off the Gold Standard.

The actress Jayne Mansfield is born in Bryn Mawr, Pennsylvania (died 1967).

Thursday 20: The term 'Gulag' first comes into use in the USSR to describe a forced labour camp. The word derives from the initial letters of the Russian phrase 'General Directorate of Camps.'

Friday 21: Rudolf Hess is appointed Deputy Fuhrer of Germany.

Saturday 22: Henry Royce, co-founder of Rolls-Royce cars, dies aged 70.

Sunday 23: Achille Varzi of Italy wins the Monaco Grand Prix motor race.

Monday 24: The German government begins persecution of the Jehovah's Witness sect.

Tuesday 25: The songwriter Jerry Leiber who with Mike Stoller goes on to pen hits such as *Hound Dog* and *Jailhouse Rock* is born in Baltimore (died 2011).

Wednesday 26: The German secret state police, the Geheime Staatspolizei ('Gestapo' for short) is formed.

Thursday 27: The first John Lewis department store opens outside London, in Nottingham.

Above; singer Willie Nelson is born on 29 Apri.l

Friday 28: The last newspaper article to be critical of the Nazi regime is published in Berlin's *Deutsche Allgemeine Zeitung.*

Saturday 29: Everton defeats Manchester City 3-0 in the FA Cup Final held at Wembley Stadium, London.

The country and western singer Willie Nelson is born in Abbott, Texas.

Sunday 30: Luis Miguel Sanchez Cerro, President of Peru, is assassinated.

Luis MIguel Sanchez Cerro is assassinated on 30 April.

The Austrian Parliament holds its last session until after the Second World War, voting to allow the country's president to rule by decree.

Winifred Drinkwater, the world's first female commercial pilot begins service, with Midland and Scottish Air Ferries Ltd.

May
1933

Monday 1: 71 die when tornadoes hit the southeastern USA.

Tuesday 2: Nazi paramilitaries stage attacks on Marxist-aligned organisations throughout Germany.

Wednesday 3: The Irish Parliament abolishes the Oath of Allegiance to the British crown.

The soul singer James Brown is born in Barnwell, South Carolina (died 2006).

Thursday 4: The Chinese dissident author Ting Ling is imprisoned.

Li Ching-Yuen, reputed to be the world's oldest man, dies on 5 May at the supposed age of 256.

Friday 5: Karl Jansky's discovery of extra-terrestrial radio waves is announced, beginning the era of radio astronomy.

The celebrated herbalist Li Ching-Yuen of Sichuan, China, dies at a reputed age of 256. Scientists dispute the claim, citing photographic evidence that he appeared to be in his late seventies when he died.

May 1933

Saturday 6: Broker's Tip wins the Kentucky Derby, ridden by Donald Meade.

Sunday 7: US President Roosevelt gives his second nationally broadcast 'fireside chat' radio address.

Monday 8: Mahatma Gandhi begins a fast in protest at the treatment of Untouchables.

Tuesday 9: The romantic novelist Jessica Steele is born in Royal Leamington Spa, Warwickshire (died 2020).

Saud bin Abdul Aziz becomes Crown Prince of Saudi Arabia on 11 May.

The Nazi party announces plans for a German national church, for Aryans only, based in Wittenberg.

Wednesday 10: German students begin a book-burning campaign.

Paraguay declares war on Bolivia, the first declaration of war by any country in the world since 1918.

The novelist Barbara Taylor Bradford (*A Woman of Substance*) is born in Leeds, Yorkshire.

Thursday 11: Saud bin Abdul Aziz is proclaimed Crown Prince of Saudi Arabia.

54 die when tornadoes hit Tennessee and Kentucky.

Friday 12: The US government gains the power to raise farm prices and and provide relief on farm mortgages.

Left: Mahatma Gandhi begins a hunger strike on 8 May.

May 1933

Saturday 13: The waxwork of Adolf Hitler in London's Madame Tussaud's is vandalised with red paint and a sign reading 'mass murderer'; the culprit is fined £5/10/-.

Sunday 14: The League of Nations affirms the historic neutrality of Switzerland.

Monday 15: In secret talks, Adolf Hitler confirms that he will not allow the restoration of the German monarchy under the exiled Kaiser Wilhelm II.

Tuesday 16: Lady Cynthia Mosley, wife of the British fascist leader Sir Oswald Mosley, dies of appendicitis aged 34.

Wednesday 17: Spain puts the Roman Catholic church under state control and bans church schools.

The Norwegian Nazi party under Vidkun Quisling is formed.

The film *I Cover the Waterfront* starring Ben Lyon and Claudette Colbert is released.

Thursday 18: One of the most ambitious programmes of US President Roosevelt's 'New Deal' begins as the Tennessee Valley Authority is set up to develop hydro-electric power.

Friday 19: The philosopher Edward de Bono, originator of the term 'lateral thinking', is born in Malta (died 2021).

Saturday 20: Japanese bombers stage a mock raid on the Chinese capital Peking, dropping leaflets warning that they will attack properly if the Japanese occupation of northeast China is opposed.

The legendary racehorse Seabiscuit, shown here with trainer Tom Smith, is born on 23 May

Sunday 21: Italian leader Benito Mussolini holds talks in Rome with British, French and German diplomats on a possible peace treaty between the four nations.

Monday 22: Tsengeltiin Jigjidav, former Prime Minister of Mongolia, is assassinated.

Joan Collins is born on 23 May.

Tuesday 23: The actress Dame Joan Collins is born in London.

The champion racing horse Seabiscuit is born in Paris, Kentucky (died 1947).

Wednesday 24: The composer Dimitri Shostakovich's 24 Preludes is first performed, in Moscow, USSR.

Thursday 25: Chinese and Japanese forces agree to a truce in northern China.

Friday 26: The singer Jimmie Rodgers, known as the 'father of country music' dies aged 35.

Saturday 27: The 1933 World's Fair opens in Chicago.

The Walt Disney 'Silly Symphonies' cartoon *The Three Little Pigs* is released.

Left: a scene from Disney's *The Three Little Pigs*, released on 27 May.

May 1933

Sunday 28: Mahatma Gandhi ends a three week fast in protest against the treatment of the Dalit (Untouchable) caste in India.

Monday 29: The Standard Oil company of America (now Chevron) signs a deal with Saudi Arabia to dig for oil. Oil is discovered in 1938.

Tuesday 30: Louis Meyer wins the Indianapolis 500 motor car race.

Wednesday 31: The Sino-Japanese ceasefire of 25 May is formalised as the Tanggu Truce; China cedes Manchuria to the Japanese puppet state of Manchukuo.

The Chrysler Motors exhibition hall at the Chicago World's Fair. The event opens on 27 May.

Chinese and Japanese generals sign the Tanggu Truce on 31 May.

June
1933

Thursday 1: The German government announces a loan of 1000 marks to any married couple if the woman gives up work; the debt is to be reduced by 25% every time the couple has a child.

Friday 2: German Jews are banned from participation in youth, welfare and sporting organisations.

Saturday 3: The President of Spain, Niceto Alcala-Zamora, is excommunicated by the Roman Catholic Church for passing a law nationalising church property.

Sunday 4: The commercial radio station aimed at British listeners, Radio Luxembourg, begins broadcasting. It is the second off-shore rival to the BBC's monopoly of the airwaves, since Radio Normandy began in 1931.

Above: the world's first drive-in movie theatre opens on 6 June.

June 1933

Above: Boxer Max Baer (shown here with actress Myrna Loy) knocks out German fighter Max Schmeling on 8 June.

Monday 5: Following the US departure from the Gold Standard, Congress nullifies the right of creditors to demand payment in gold.

Tuesday 6: The world's first permanent drive-in movie theatre opens in Pennsauken Township, New Jersey.

Wednesday 7: Representatives of Britain, France, Germany and Italy sign the Four Power Pact peace treaty in Rome. The agreement pledges a decade of peace and disarmament.

Thursday 8: In a match said to have embarrassed Nazi Party supporters, Hitler's favourite boxer Max Schmeling is knocked out by the half-Jewish fighter Max Baer in front of 60,000 spectators at the Yankee Stadium in New York City.

Above: Gene Wilder is born on 11 June.

Friday 9: The first test rocket launch of the Magdeburg Project, a German plan for eventual manned space travel, ends in failure.

Saturday 10: 50 die when the Taurus Express passenger train crashes between Istanbul and Adana, Turkey.

Sunday 11: The actor Gene Wilder is born in Milwaukee, Wisconsin (died 2016).

Monday 12: Representatives of 64 nations meet in London as part of the 1933 World Economic Conference on monetary policy, trade and war reparations.

June 1933

Gangster Charles Pretty Boy Floyd shoots four policemen on 17 June.

Tuesday 13: The British government announces it will partially default on its war debt repayments to the USA.

Wednesday 14: While attempting the first solo flight around the world, US pilot Jimmie Mattern crash lands in Siberia. He is eventually rescued by Eskimos two weeks later.

Thursday 15: Finland is announced as the only European country to not have defaulted on war debts to the USA.

Friday 16: The Zionist leader Haim Arlosoroff is assassinated in Tel Aviv, British Palestine (now Israel).

Saturday 17: Four police officers are killed in a shoot-out with the notorious gangster Charles 'Pretty Boy' Floyd in Kansas City, Missouri.

Sunday 18: The Chinese civil rights leader Yang Quan is assassinated in Shanghai.

Monday 19: The Austrian Nazi Party is outlawed, following a series of bomb attacks which are attributed to them.

The exiled Crown Prince Alfonso, heir to the throne of Spain, is married to Edelmira Sampedro in Lausanne, Switzerland.

Tuesday 20: The USSR's Belomor Canal, linking the White Sea to the Baltic is completed, while in the USA, the Illinois Waterway is opened, connecting the Great Lakes with the Gulf of Mexico.

Right: Barbara Hutton, the Woolworth heiress, is married on 20 June.

June 1933

Bernie Kopell (shown here in 1977) is born on 21 June.

The government of Siam (now Thailand) is overthrown in a bloodless coup led by the Colonel Phraya Phahonphonphayauhasena, who later shortens his name to Phot Phahonyothin.

The socialite Barbara Hutton marries the exiled Prince Alexis Mdivani of Georgia.

Wednesday 21: The actor Bernie Kopell (*The Love Boat*) is born in New York City.

The Nazi Party in Germany bans the paramilitary wing of its political allies, the Nationalist Party.

Thursday 22: The Nazi Party's rival, the Social Democratic Party of Germany, is outlawed.

Friday 23: Barney Ross defeats Tony Canzoneri to win the World Lightweight Boxing championship in Chicago.

Saturday 24: The Italian Air Force launches a flotilla of 24 aircraft to cross the Atlantic, with the destination of the Chicago World's Fair.

Sunday 25: Martial law is declared in Bulgaria following the discovery of a communist plot to overthrow the government.

Monday 26: 1150 people are arrested and 200 bombs seized in Bulgaria as troops conduct house to house searches for the ringleaders of the communist coup attempt.

Louise Arner Boyd sets sail for Greenland on 28 June.

Tuesday 27: The German National Party is outlawed by its former allies the Nazis.

Comedy actor Fatty Arbuckle dies on 18 June.

The German autobahn programme goes into operation with the setting up of a nationalised roads company.

Wednesday 28: The American explorer Louise Arner Boyd begins leading the Veslekari Expedition to northern Greenland.

Thursday 29: Italy's Primo Carnera becomes the world heavyweight boxing champion after defeating Jack Sharkey in New York City.

The silent comedian Roscoe 'Fatty' Arbuckle dies aged 46, the day after accepting a starring role in what was intended as his come-back film following a ten-year absence from the screen.

Friday 30: The Screen Actors' Guild is set up as the trade union for American film actors.

July
1933

Saturday 1: The London Transport Passenger Board is formed, bringing all of London's public transport under one body.

The Douglas DC-1 airliner makes its first flight.

Adolf Hitler quashes rumours that he is about to join the new Nazi state church, stating that he is a Roman Catholic and will remain so.

Sunday 2: An assassination attempt is made on King Carol II of Romania in Cluj; the monarch is unharmed.

Monday 3: The US government announces that the dollar will remain off the Gold Standard for the foreseeable future.

Tuesday 4: The Convention for the Definition of Aggression, an international peace treaty between several League of Nations countries, is signed in London.

Left: The Douglas DC-1 first flies on 1 July.

July 1933

Left: an AEC Regent, the standard London bus of the early 1930s. On 1 July, control of the capital's buses passes from the General Omnibus Company to the newly formed London Transport.

Wednesday 5: The Catholic Centre Party, the only remaining opposition party in Germany, votes to disband.

Thursday 6: The first Major League Baseball All-Star Game, also known as the Midsummer Classic, is played in Chicago to raise funds for retired players.

Friday 7: The oldest regular major league baseball player in the USA, Jack Quinn, retires aged 50.

Amelia Earhart flies across the USA on 8 July.

Saturday 8: The pilot Amelia Earhart sets an air speed record when she completes a crossing of the continental USA in 17 hours and 7 minutes.

Sunday 9: The international Convention for Limiting the Manufacture and Regulating the Distribution of Narcotic Drugs comes into effect.

Monday 10: A bomb plot to overthrow the government of Japan and install the Emperor's younger brother in his place is foiled at the last minute by Tokyo police.

July 1933

Popeye makes his first screen appearance on 14 July.

Tuesday 11: The German government bans the use of the name Hitler as a Christian name for children.

Wednesday 12: A newspaper in Vienna reveals that Adolf Hitler is part-Jewish (one-sixteenth) on his mother's side.

Thursday 13: The greeting 'Heil Hitler' and the Nazi salute are made compulsory for all German government employees.

The novelist David Storey (*This Sporting Life*) is born in Wakefield, Yorkshire.

The Ski Club of Great Britain abolishes the term 'ski-runner' and 'ski-running' and replaces it with 'ski-er' and 'ski-ing'.

Friday 14: Germany begins compulsory sterilisation of persons with certain hereditary diseases.

The cartoon character Popeye makes his first screen appearance with the release of the animated film *Popeye the Sailor.*

Franz, Duke of Bavaria, heir to the House of Stuart and nominal head of the Jacobite cause, is born in Munich.

Saturday 15: Representatives of Britain, France, Germany and Italy sign the Four Power Pact pledging peace for ten years.

Berlin academics give the Nazi salute. The greeting is made compulsory for all state employees on 13 July.

Pilot Wiley Post completes the first solo flight around the world on 22 July.

Sunday 16: Work begins on the Grand Coulee Dam in Washington State.

The shipping magnate Sir John Ellerman, reputed to be Britain's richest man, dies aged 71.

Monday 17: The work-week of US cotton mill workers is reduced from 54 hours to 40, with no reduction in pay.

Tuesday 18: Edwin H Land, who goes on to invent the Polaroid camera, is granted a US patent for polarizing film.

Wednesday 19: The 22-year-old actress Lucille Ball signs her first motion picture contract to appear in the Eddie Cantor film *Roman Scandals.*

Thursday 20: The German government signs an agreement with the Vatican that Roman Catholic canon law will not be interfered with in Germany. In exchange the Vatican agrees to discourage priests from political activity.

Friday 21: Fr Charles Uncles, the USA's first black Roman Catholic priest, dies aged 74.

Saturday 22: Wiley Post becomes the first pilot to fly solo around the world, completing the trip in 7 days 18 hours 45 minutes.

Above: gangsters Bonnie and Clyde narrowly avoid capture on 24 July.

Sunday 23: The German Evangelical Church, a grouping of Protestant denominations broadly in support of the Nazi Party, is set up.

July 1933

London's Battersea Power Station goes into operation on 26 July.

Monday 24: The notorious gangsters Bonnie and Clyde (Bonnie Parker and Clyde Barrow) narrowly avoid capture in a shoot-out with police in Dexter, Iowa.

Tuesday 25: France claims the Spratly Islands in the Pacific Ocean as part of French Indochina.

Wednesday 26: The overthrow of the Cuban government of Gerado Machado begins with a strike action campaign.

London's Battersea Power Station goes into operation.

Thursday 27: The World Economic Conference ends with a commitment by the countries of the British Empire to remain off the Gold Standard.

Friday 28: Western Union introduces the 'singing telegram', where a message, usually for a birthday, is sung by the deliverer.

The Grand Jury – a group of citizens engaged to investigate criminal cases – is abolished in English law.

Saturday 29: J Edgar Hoover is reappointed as head of the US Federal Bureau of Investigation (FBI) a post he holds until his death in 1972.

Dizzy Dean breaks baseball records on 30 July.

J Edgar Hoover takes over the FBI on 29 July.

Sunday 30: Baseball player Dizzy Dean of the St Louis Cardinals sets the record for the highest number of strike-outs (17) in one game to this date.

Monday 31: The long-running US radio serial *Jack Armstrong the All American Boy* is first broadcast.

Mahatma Gandhi announces a campaign of individual civil disobedience against British rule in India.

August
1933

Tuesday 1: Gandhi is arrested on charges of sedition and sent to Yervadi Jail in Poona. On the same day, the Indonesian independence leader Sukarno is imprisoned by Dutch colonial authorities.

Wednesday 2: The 114 mile-long White Sea Baltic Canal is opened, linking the White Sea with the Baltic via Lake Onega.

Thursday 3: The comedian and amateur astronomer Will Hay is the first person to see the third known occurrence of the Great White Spot of Saturn, a periodic meteorological event which forms huge clouds in the planet's upper atmosphere.

Left: the Great White Spot of Saturn (photographed here in 2011) is first reported by the comedian and amateur astronomer Will Hay (above) on 3 August.

August 1933

Friday 4: A tear gas attack forces the closure of the New York Stock Exchange; a disgruntled Boston lawyer is thought to be responsible for the outrage.

Saturday 5: The exotic dancer Sally Rand is arrested for performing a 'nude' dance in Chicago; it is later revealed that the 'nudity' was an optical illusion created by the skilful use of two hand fans.

Sunday 6: New York lawyer Samuel Untermeyer launches a nationwide US boycott campaign against German goods due to the anti-semitic policies of the Nazi Party.

Helen Jacobs wins the
US Open on 10 August.

Monday 7: Iraqi troops massacre up to 600 civilians of the Assyrian Christian minority at Simele.

The French pilots Paul Codos and Maurice Rossi set a record for the longest non-stop flight, travelling 5,700 miles from New York City to Rayak, Syria, in 59 hours.

Tuesday 8: As tensions rise in Cuba, US Ambassador Sumner Welles, attempts to persuade the unpopular President Gerado Machado to step down; Machado refuses.

Wednesday 9: President Machado of Cuba declares the country to be in a state of war and orders troops to defend the capital Havana from insurrectionists.

Thursday 10: Helen Jacobs wins the US Open tennis championships when she defeats Helen Wills Moody in Forest Hills, New York.

Left: President Machado of Cuba.

August 1933

Above: Gene Sarazen wins the PGA championships on 13 August.

Friday 11: The Cuban armed forces mutiny, refusing to follow the orders of President Machado and ordering him to stand down.

Saturday 12: Winston Churchill makes his first speech warning of the dangers of German re-armament.

Cuba's President Machado flees the country, as rampaging mobs attack his palace. He is replaced by Carlos Manuel de Cespedes.

Sunday 13: Gene Sarazen wins the PGA golf championships at Wauwatosa, Wisconsin.

As the Cuban uprising continues, USS *Claxton* and *Taylor* are despatched to evacuate US citizens from the island.

Monday 14: A major forest fire known as the Tillamook Burn begins in Oregon, USA; it lasts for nearly three weeks and destroys 311,000 acres of woodland.

Tuesday 15: The folk singer Mike Seeger is born in New York City (died 2009).

The German government announces 'relentless' measures against communist activity, including the imprisonment of innocent relatives of political activists.

Lou Gehrig makes baseball history on 17 August.

Wednesday 16: Major rioting breaks out in Toronto, Canada, between pro-Nazi and Jewish groups.

The imprisoned Indian nationalist leader Mahatma Gandhi announces a 'fast unto death' against British rule.

Thursday 17: The first Soviet rocket, the GIRD 109, is launched, reaching a maximum altitude thought to be around one mile.

The film *The Private Life of Henry VIII*, starring Charles Laughton is released. It goes on to become the first British film to win an Academy Award.

Baseball player Lou Gehrig of the New York Yankees sets a record for the highest number of games played (1308). He goes on to play another 822, a record which remains unbroken until 1995.

Friday 18: The gangster Lester Gillis, better known as 'Baby Face Nelson' makes his first bank robbery, escaping with $14,000 in Grand Haven, Michigan.

The film director Roman Polanksi is born in Paris, France.

Saturday 19: As part of US President Roosevelt's 'New Deal' to beat unemployment, a programme of hiring 40,000 teachers for rural schools is announced.

Sunday 20: The Indian nationalist leader Mahatma Gandhi, still on hunger strike, is transferred from prison to hospital in Poona.

Monday 21: Sheila Borrett becomes the first female newsreader on BBC radio.

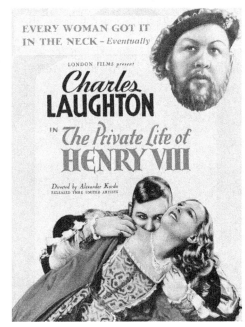

Above: Charles Laughton stars in *The Private Life of Henry VIII*, released on 17 August.

August 1933

Tuesday 22: Austria's chancellor Englebert Dollfuss asks the Western Allies for permission under the Treaty of Versailles to increase the strength of his army due to fears of encroaching Nazi paramilitary activity on the border with Germany.

Wednesday 23: The German government begins publishing lists of those whose citizenship has been revoked, including authors Heinrich Mann and Ernst Toller.

Thursday 24: At least 42 people are feared dead when a major storm hits the eastern seaboard of the northeastern USA.

Friday 25: 9300 die in the Diexi Earthquake in Sichuan, China.

Saturday 26: Texas becomes the twenty-third US state to repeal Prohibition.

The largest tuna fish on record, weighing 1050 pounds, is caught by Captain Joseph Penny off the coast of Nova Scotia; it beats the previous 700 lb record held by the writer Zane Grey.

Sunday 27: The Haavara Agreement goes into effect in Germany, allowing Jews to migrate to Palestine without

A German Jewish town under construction in British Mandatory Palestine (now Israel). German migrants flock to the area after the Haavara Agreement of 27 August.

interference. 60,000 German Jews leave on the scheme, which continues until the outbreak of war in 1939.

Monday 28: The US government bans private ownership of gold certificates and coins.

Ethel 'Sunny' Lowry of Manchester becomes the second British woman to swim the English Channel, in 15 hours 41 minutes.

Tuesday 29: Gold mining is nationalised in the USA.

The *New York Times* breaks the news of Germany's growing number of concentration camps.

Baseball legend Babe Ruth announces his retirement on 31 August.

Wednesday 30: The German writer Theodor Lessing is assassinated in Czechoslovakia after criticising the Nazi regime.

Thursday 31: The baseball player George 'Babe' Ruth announces his retirement.

September 1933

Friday 1: The romantic comedy film *One Sunday Afternoon* starring Gary Cooper and Fay Wray is released.

The country music singer Conway Twitty is born in Friar's Point, Mississippi (died 1993).

Saturday 2: The long-running weekly British story-paper for children, the *Hotspur*, is first published.

Sunday 3: The Irish political party *Fine Gael* is created.

Monday 4: Pilot Jimmy Wedell sets the over-land air speed record at an average of over 300 mph at the National Air Races in Chicago. The event is marred by tragedy as 29 year old pilot Florence Klingensmith, the first woman contender for the race, is killed when her plane crashes at 200 mph.

Hotspur **is first published on 2 September.**

Tuesday 5: Cuba's provisional President Carlos Cespedes, in power for less than a week, is pushed aside by the 'Revolt of the Sergeants' a coup led by future President Fulgencio Batista.

Above: Jimmy Wedell (inset) sets the world air speed record on 4 September in a Wedell-Williams 44 aeroplane.

Wednesday 6: A regiment of US Marines are put on stand-by to restore order in Cuba.

Thursday 7: 16 US Navy destroyers are despatched to Cuba.

Sir Edward Grey, Britain's Foreign Secretary during the First World War, dies aged 71.

Friday 8: King Faisal I of Iraq dies aged 48; he is succeeded by his son, Crown Prince Ghazi.

The playwright and novelist Michael Frayn is born in London.

Saturday 9: 15 year-old Marion Bergeron of Connecticut becomes the youngest woman to win the Miss America beauty pageant in Atlantic City, New Jersey.

Sunday 10: Dr Ramon Grau becomes the fourth President of Cuba within a month.

Monday 11: The Austrian dictator Englbert Dollfuss proclaims the one-party Federal State of Austria, which lasts until German annexation in 1938.

Tuesday 12: The physicist Leó Szilárd conceives the idea of

September 1933

Above: poster for the film *The Emperor Jones*, released on 19 September.

nuclear fission while waiting for a traffic light to change in London. The sequence of coloured lights inspires him to begin work on creating an atomic chain reaction.

Wednesday 13: Elizabeth Combs becomes the first woman to be elected to the New Zealand Parliament.

The drama film *Berkeley Square* starring Leslie Howard and Heather Angel is released.

Thursday 14: Troops are sent to the city of Serowe in the colony of British Bechuanaland, to depose King Tshekedi of the Bamangwato tribe after he permitted the flogging of an Englishman in a native court.

Friday 15: An international legal commission investigating the Reichstag fire in Berlin hears evidence suggesting it was caused by an arson attack by Nazi Party members.

Saturday 16: The Columbia News Service, forerunner of the USA's CBS News, is founded.

Sunday 17: German Nazi Party members stage a riot in Graz, Austria, where their organisation is outlawed.

Hollywood's 'Blonde Bombshell' Jean Harlow marries for the third time on 18 September.

At least 15 people are killed and millions of dollars worth of damage caused when fierce storms lash the coast of the northeastern USA.

September 1933

Monday 18: The film star Jean Harlow marries her third husband, cameraman Harold Rosson, in Yuma, Arizona.

Tuesday 19: The film *The Emperor Jones*, starring Paul Robeson, is released.

The actor David McCallum (*The Man from UNCLE*) is born in Glasgow.

Wednesday 20: Record-breaking numbers of Jews attend Jewish New Year services at German synagogues in defiance of the government's anti-semitic legislation.

David McCallum (shown here in 1964) is born on 19 September.

The political activist and Theosophist Annie Besant, acampaigner for womens' rights and Indian independence, dies aged 85.

Thursday 21: The USSR founds the Reactive Scientific Research Institute to develop rocket technology.

Friday 22: The notorious US bank robber John Dillinger is arrested at a boarding house in Dayton, Ohio.

Saturday 23: Adolf Hitler turns the first spadeful of earth as construction begins on the first autobahn (motorway), from Frankfurt to Darmstadt.

Far left: gangster Machine Gun Kelly is arrested on 26 September; bank robber John Dillinger (left) is captured on 26 September.

September 1933

Sunday 24: The nuclear physicist Klaus Fuchs arrives in England after fleeing Nazi persecution in Germany. He goes on to work on the Allied atomic bomb programme and is later convicted of passing atomic secrets to the Russians.

Monday 25: Up to 5000 people are killed when a hurricane hits the town of Tampico, Mexico.

Tuesday 26: The notorious gangster George 'Machine Gun' Kelly is captured by the FBI in Memphis, Tennessee.

Marilyn Miller stars in the musical *As Thousands Cheer* which opens on 30 September.

Wednesday 27: Ludwig Müller is elected as the first bishop of the *Reichskirche*, the newly formed German state church approved by the Nazi Party.

Thursday 28: French pilot Gustav Lemoine sets an altitude record of 44,819 feet (8.5 miles/13,611 metres) in a Potez 33 aeroplane.

Friday 29: Ernest Holloway Oldham, a cipher clerk in the London Foreign Office, commits suicide after being caught passing secrets to the Soviets.

Saturday 30: Irving Berlin's musical *As Thousands Cheer* opens on Broadway, featuring the hit songs *Easter Parade* and *Heatwave*.

October
1933

Sunday 1: 33 people are killed when the Japanese sightseeing boat *Koun Maru* capsizes off the coast at Kumamoto.

King Te Rata Mahuta, King of the Maoris, dies aged 56.

Monday 2: The Eugene O'Neill play *Ah, Wilderness* opens in New York City.

Tuesday 3: The Austrian dictator Englebert Dollfuss survives an assassination attempt.

Wednesday 4: The press in Germany is brought under full control of the government; non-Aryans are banned from working as newspaper and magazine editors.

Thursday 5: Britain's Labour Party, during its

Above: *I'm No Angel* starring Cary Grant and Mae West is released on 6 October.

Esquire magazine is first published on 15 October.

annual conference, passes a resolution that no member will be involved in war.

Friday 6: At the Conservative Party Conference, leader Stanley Baldwin calls for a disarmament convention.

Britain's Milk Marketing Board is established.

The film *I'm No Angel* starring Mae West is released.

Saturday 7: Air France is formed by the merger of five French airlines.

Sunday 8: Diego Martinez Barrio becomes Prime Minister of Spain.

Koroki Mahuta is crowned King of the Maoris in New Zealand.

Monday 9: The physicist Sir Peter Mansfield is born in London.

Tuesday 10: The first bomb attack on an airliner takes place when a United Airlines Boeing 247 explodes over Chesterton, Indiana. All seven on board are killed and the bomber is never identified.

Wednesday 11: Britain, the USA and France agree to refuse Germany's request to re-arm.

Thursday 12: The notorious criminal John Dillinger is broken out of jail in Lima, Ohio, by members of his gang who kill a Sheriff, Jesse Sarber, in the raid.

Friday 13: The romantic comedy *Blonde Bombshell* starring Jean Harlow and Lee Tracy is released.

October 1933

Saturday 14: Germany announces it is withdrawing from the League of Nations following the refusal of its request to re-arm.

Above: the Grumman F2F fighter first flies on 18 October.

Sunday 15: The first issue of *Esquire* magazine is published in the USA.

The Rolls Royce Merlin engine, later used in the iconic Spitfire and Hurricane fighter planes of the RAF, is tested for the first time.

Monday 16: The airship USS *Macon* completes a transcontinental trip from Lakehurst, New Jersey, to Sunnyfield, California.

Tuesday 17: Albert Einstein arrives in the USA as an exile from Nazi Germany.

Wednesday 18: The Grumman F2F fighter aeroplane makes its first flight.

Thursday 19: The US Government begins informal talks with the USSR over establishing diplomatic relations.

The airship USS *Macon* crosses the USA on 16 October.

October 1933

Friday 20: Guglielmo Marconi, pioneer of wireless, announces that television will never supplant radio because 'sending sound is more important to mankind to sending sight.'

Saturday 21: The George and Ira Gershwin musical *Let 'Em Eat Cake* opens on Broadway; it turns out to be a relative flop, closing after 89 performances.

Left: Turin's modernist Mussolini Stadium under construction. The venue opens on 28 October.

Sunday 22: Iceland repeals Prohibition, in place since 1915.

Monday 23: On the same day two notorious bank robbers carry out raids in the USA: John Dillinger in Greencastle, Indiana, and Baby Face Nelson in Brainerd, Minnesota.

Tuesday 24: Édouard Deladier resigns as Prime Minister of France; he is replaced by Albert Sarraut.

The gangster twins Ronald and Reginald Kray are born in London (died 1995 and 2000 respectively).

Wednesday 25: The US radio soap opera *Dangerous Paradise* begins on CBS Radio.

Thursday 26: The Indiana National Guard (state militia) is called out to find the bank robber gang led by John Dillinger; the gang flees to Chicago.

Friday 27: The Anglo-Japanese trade alliance is renewed in a conference held in Simla, India.

Left: a souvenir postcard of the original Anglo-Japanese Alliance of 1905. The agreement is renewed on 27 October.

Saturday 28: The Mussolini Stadium is opened in Turin, Italy.

Sunday 29: Two people are killed and 60 injured when fighting breaks out between the Arab and Jewish populations in Jerusalem, British Mandatory Palestine (now Israel).

Monday 30: The Spanish fascist organisation Falange Espanola is formed under Jose Antonio Primo de Rivera.

Jerusalem is put under the control of British troops as disturbances continue between Arabs and Jews.

Tuesday 31: The exiled German composer Arnold Schoenberg arrives in the USA.

Left: British colonial police launch a baton charge against rioters in Jerusalem, 27 October.

November 1933

Wednesday 1: The US First Lady, Eleanor Roosevelt's book on household management, *It's Up To The Women* is published.

Thursday 2: Home rule in the British colony of Malta is suspended after the National Party advocates Italian as an official language in order to align the island more closely with Mussolini's regime.

Friday 3: The actor Jeremy Brett (Sherlock Holmes) is born in Berkswell, Warwickshire (died 1995).

The composer John Barry, famous for his James Bond film themes, is born in York (died 2011).

Saturday 4: Britain's Parliament discusses the growing problem of the Muskrat; the rodent population is said to have reached serious levels in Shropshire and Montgomeryshire.

Above: the Muskrat. Parliament debates the growing problem of the invasive species on 4 November.

Left: a 'dustbowl' storm in Texas. The first of these types of storms is in South Dakota on 11 November.

Sunday 5: The Battle of Fort Arce takes place in the war between Paraguay and Bolivia.

Monday 6: Portuguese dictator Antonio de Oliveira Salazar establishes special military courts to counter subversion and industrial action.

Tuesday 7: Mahatma Gandhi begins a nine-month tour of India to promote the cause of the Untouchable caste.

Wednesday 8: King Mohammed Nadir Shah of Afghanistan is assassinated.

Thursday 9: William Dick, an American Indian thought to be the last native speaker of the Mohican language, dies aged 76.

The Civil Works Administration, a job creation scheme, is launched in the USA as part of President Roosevelt's New Deal.

Friday 10: Four people are killed when a United Airlines plane crashes in fog near Portland, Oregon.

Saturday 11: The first major 'dust bowl' storm takes place in South Dakota, USA. A feature of the Great Depression, the storms strip the topsoil from agricultural land, causing it to

November 1933

Left: the first photograph of what is claimed to be the Loch Ness Monster is taken on 12 November by Hugh Gray. Some experts denounce it as a fake, saying it shows a dog with a branch in its mouth; others suggest it shows a large eel.

become infertile and leading to the mass exodus of farmers from the midwest.

Governance of Easter Island is transferred from a private company to the Republic of Chile.

The first commercially made 'Girl Scout Cookies' are sold in Philadelphia, Pennsylvania, to commemorate Armistice Day.

Sunday 12: Germany withdraws from the League of Nations following a referendum.

The Canon photographic company is founded in Tokyo, Japan.

Hugh Gray becomes the first person to photograph what is claimed to be the Loch Ness Monster. Mr Gray, a local man, says he saw a creature of 'considerable size' with a tail moving around in the water. Experts remain divided on what the photograph really shows; some say it is just a fish and others a dog swimming with a branch in its mouth.

Monday 13: The science fiction film *The Invisible Man* starring Claude Rains is released.

Right: the Kwanon, Japan's first 35mm camera, goes into production after the Canon company is founded on 12 November.

At the first rally of the new pro-Nazi state church, the *Reichskirche,* speaker Reinhold Krause announces the Jewish Old Testament has 'no meaning for the Nordic race.'

Above: Claude Rains stars in *The Invisible Man*, released on 13 November.

Tuesday 14: Benito Mussolini dissolves the Italian Parliament's Chamber of Deputies, replacing it with a fascist-aligned 'National Guild Council' of corporations.

Wednesday 15: The first democratic elections in the history of Siam (Thailand) take place.

All 27 crew of the British freighter *Saxilby* are lost when the ship goes down in the Irish Sea.

Thursday 16: The USA and USSR establish diplomatic relations.

The world's highest waterfall, Angel Falls in Venezuela, is discovered by pilot Jimmie Angel.

The film *Little Women* starring Katharine Hepburn and Joan Bennet is released.

Left: The Marx Brothers' comedy *Duck Soup* is released on 17 November

November 1933

Above: *Century of Progress* breaks the world altitude record on 20 November.

Friday 17: William C Bullitt is appointed as the first American ambassador to the USSR, with Alexander Troyanovsky as his Soviet counterpart.

The Marx Brothers comedy film *Duck Soup* is released.

Saturday 18: Japanese troops clash with Korean nationalists on the border of China and North Korea.

Sunday 19: Alejandro Lerroux forms a coalition government in Spain following a general election, the first in which women are allowed to vote.

The US talk show host Larry King is born in New York City (died 2021).

Monday 20: The US Navy balloon, *Century of Progress* piloted by Jean Piccard ascends to a record height of 61,000 feet/11.5 miles (18,592 metres).

Tuesday 21: The novelist Beryl Bainbridge (*An Awfully Big Adventure*) is born in Liverpool (died 2010).

Wednesday 22: A Labour Member of Parliament, John McGovern, causes outrage when he hurls abuse at King George V and Queen Mary during the state opening, calling them 'lazy parasites'.

The gangsters Bonnie and Clyde are injured while escaping an arrest attempt near Sowers, Texas.

Thursday 23: The captains of England's county cricket teams vote to ban the 'bodyline' bowling technique (intented to intimidate the batsman into a weaker defensive stroke).

November 1933

Friday 24: Adolf Hitler introduces strict animal welfare laws in Germany.

Saturday 25: The USSR launches the GIRD-X experimental rocket, which ascends to a height of 262 feet (80 metres).

Sunday 26: The Seventh Day Adventist denomination is banned in Germany; the ban is later lifted on the understanding that the church will not criticise the Nazi regime.

Herman Goering takes over the Gestapo on 30 November.

Monday 27: As the end of Prohibition nears, the US government takes over temporary control of the liquor industry to prevent 'confusion and uncertainty' until new laws are passed.

Tuesday 28: The biggest Van der Graff generator built to this date generates seven million volts of electricity during demonstration to the public in Cambridge, Massachusetts.

Wednesday 29: Three prisoners make a daring break-out from the 'unescapable' French penal colony of Devil's Island near French Guiana. The incident forms the basis of the book and film *Papillion*.

Thursday 30: Herman Goering announces that the Gestapo (German secret police) will come under his personal control.

December
1933

Friday 1: Amid rumours that he wants to create a united Ireland, Eamon de Valera, President of the Irish Free State, wins a seat in the Northern Ireland Parliament. He cannot however serve as an MP due to his refusal to swear the Loyal Oath.

Saturday 2: In a Los Angeles court, bootlegger Frank Cornero and his sister Catherine become the last persons to be convicted under Prohibition laws in the USA. The nationwide alcohol ban is withdrawn on 5 December.

Above: Bernadette Soubirou (St Bernadette of Lourdes) is canonised on 8 December

Sunday 3: The Public Works administration of the USA announces that three million government jobs have been created in the drive to reduce unemployment.

Monday 4: The most popular play of the 1930s, *Tobacco Road* is first performed. It closes in 1941, making it the longest running Broadway show until superceded by *Life With Father* in 1947.

Tuesday 5: The 21st Amendment to the Constitution – the repeal of Prohibition – comes into force in the USA. The alcohol ban, in place since 1920, had become difficult and costly to enforce and was unpopular with voters.

Wednesday 6: The novel *Ullyses* by James Joyce is ruled to be not obscene, and suitable for publication in the USA, ending a 12 year ban on its importation.

Thursday 7: The best selling novel *Goodbye Mr Chips* by James Hilton is published.

Friday 8: Bernadette Soubirous, the teenage girl who in 1858 claimed to have had a vision of the Virgin Mary in Lourdes, France, is canonized.

Above: James Hilton's popular novel of school life, *Goodbye Mr Chips*, is published on 7 December.

Saturday 9: Film stars Mary Pickford and Douglas Fairbanks announce their divorce.

The German aviation pioneer Karl Jatho, famous for his (disputed) claim to have been the first man to fly an aeroplane (in 1903, three months before the Wright Brothers), dies aged 60.

Sunday 10: Romania's Prime Minister, Ion Duca, orders the dissolution of the Iron Guard, the country's fascist paramilitary organisation based on the Nazi model.

Monday 11: At least 78 people are thought to have been killed in an Anarchist revolt in Spain, as extremists clash with government troops in Barcelona, Alava, Hesca and Teruel provinces.

Tuesday 12: All German press services are merged into the German News Bureau, an offshoot of the ruling Nazi Party.

Wednesday 13: 55 people die as severe ice storms hit the northwestern USA.

December 1933

Above: roll out the barrel! New Yorkers celebrate the end of thirteen years of Prohibition on 5 December.

Thursday 14: Alexander Korsariov, head of the Communist Youth Association in Russia, announces that dancing to jazz music and wearing fashionable clothes are now permitted for Russian youth, but 'free love' and drunkenness are still taboo.

Friday 15: India hosts its first Test cricket match, after having been granted Test status in 1932. She loses to England after nine wickets.

Saturday 16: Diego Martinez Barrio resigns as Prime Minister of Spain; he is replaced by Alejandro Lerroux.

Sunday 17: In American football, the Chicago Bears defeat the New York Giants 23-21 in the first NFL Championship Game.

Thubten Gyatso, 13th Dalai Lama of Tibet, dies aged 54.

Monday 18: Yemen invades Saudi Arabia.

The German government announces a recruitment drive to

increase the strength of its armed forces to 300,000 men.

Tuesday 19: Bolivia accepts truce proposals from Paraguay, halting the Gran Chaco border war.

Wednesday 20: The first US Ambassador to the USSR, William C Bullitt, arrives in Moscow to take up his post.

Thursday 21: The Canadian island of Newfoundland is returned to direct rule by Britain.

Above: the Thirteenth Dalai Lama dies on 17 December.

Friday 22: The film *Son of Kong*, sequel to King Kong, is released.

Saturday 23: 200 people are killed when an express train collides with a local at Lagny-Sur-Marne near Paris, France.

Emperor Akihito of Japan is born in Tokyo.

Sunday 24: Pope Pius XI in his Christmas message publicly attacks the German government, particularly criticising the Nazis' sterilization programme.

Monday 25: US President Roosevelt restores citizenship to those stripped of it for opposition to the Great War. 1,500 persons convicted under the Espionage Act or charged with evasion of conscription are pardoned.

Frankie Klick becomes the World Lightweight boxing champion after knocking out Eligio Montalvo ('Kid Chocolate') in Philadelphia.

Left: Helen Mack stars in *Son of Kong*, released on 22 December.

December 1933

Above: Helen Richey, who with co-pilot Frances Marsalis breaks the record for longest flight on 30 December in their plane 'Outdoor Girl'.

Tuesday 26: Edwin H Armstrong is granted a patent for Frequency Modulation (FM) radio.

The Nissan Motor Company is formed in Tokyo, Japan.

Wednesday 27: The *Codex Sinaiticus*, the oldest complete manuscript of the New Testament dating from 360AD, is purchased by the British Museum from the USSR.

Thursday 28: President Roosevelt announces that the foreign policy of the USA will be one of opposition to armed intervention.

Friday 29: Ion Duca, Prime Minister of Romania, is assassinated by a member of the recently outlawed Iron Guard, a fascist organisation based on Germany's Nazi Party.

Saturday 30: Pilots Helen Richey and Frances Marsalis land in Miami, Florida, after setting the record for the longest aeroplane flight at 236 hours, using mid-air refueling.

Sunday 31: The USSR's Polikarpov I-16 fighter plane makes its first flight.

Other titles from
Montpelier Publishing

A Little Book of Limericks: Funny Rhymes for all the Family
ISBN 9781511524124

Scottish Jokes: A Wee Book of Clean Caledonian Chuckles
ISBN 9781495297366

The Old Fashioned Joke Book: Gags and Funny Stories
ISBN 9781514261989

Non-Religious Funeral Readings: Philosophy and Poetry for Secular Services
ISBN 9781500512835

Large Print Jokes: Hundreds of Gags in Easy-to-Read Type
ISBN 9781517775780

Spiritual Readings for Funerals and Memorial Services
ISBN 9781503379329

Victorian Murder: True Crimes, Confessions and Executions
ISBN 9781530296194

Large Print Prayers: A Prayer for Each Day of the Month
ISBN 9781523251476

A Little Book of Ripping Riddles and Confounding Conundrums
ISBN 9781505548136

Vinegar uses: over 150 ways to use vinegar
ISBN 9781512136623

Large Print Wordsearch: 100 Puzzles in Easy-to-Read Type
ISBN 9781517638894

The Pipe Smoker's Companion
ISBN 9781500441401

The Book of Church Jokes
ISBN 9781507620632

Bar Mitzvah Notebook
ISBN 9781976007781

Jewish Jokes
ISBN 9781514845769

Large Print Address Book
ISBN 9781539820031

How to Cook Without a Kitchen: Easy, Healthy and Low-Cost Meals
9781515340188

Large Print Birthday Book
ISBN 9781544670720

Retirement Jokes
ISBN 9781519206350

Take my Wife: Hilarious Jokes of Love and Marriage
ISBN 9781511790956

Welsh Jokes: A Little Book of Wonderful Welsh Wit
ISBN 9781511612241

1001 Ways to Save Money: Thrifty Tips for the Fabulously Frugal!
ISBN 9781505432534

Order online at Amazon or from your local bookshop